Bibliografische Information der Deutschen Nationalbibliothek: Die Deutsche Nationalbibliothek verzeichnet diese Publikation in der Deutschen Nationalbibliografie; detaillierte bibliografische Daten sind im Internet über http://dnb.dnb.de/ abrufbar.

© 2017 Stefan F.M. Dittrich
All rights reserved
Publisher: Stefan F.M. Dittrich – NLPLanka

www.nlp-lanka.com

Herstellung und Verlag: BoD – Books on Demand, Norderstedt

ISBN-13: 9-783743-179028

About the Author

Stefan F.M. Dittrich
Coach, Trainer and Author

Stefan F.M. Dittrich was born and raised in Germany. There he learned about NLP when he was 18 years old and realized, now it is only his responsibility to make the live he wanted.

He worked in a mental hospital for about ten years and found out, that his skills in NLP can help his patients. So he started a qualified educational program with the DVNLP (main association for NLP in Germany) and also learned hypnosis and general coaching- and therapy-methods.

As a well educated Personal- and Business-Coach Stefan Dittrich has abilities to help you and your employees reflecting strategies, processes and habits. He will give you the chance to rise and optimize performances.

Stefan also has experience as a trainer and team-leader which will enlarge your in-house competences.

Table of content

Hello and welcome to HypnoSale!	6
Hack no. 1: Rapport	9
Hack no. 2: The "like-me-Drug"	17
Hack no. 3: Fake options	20
Hack no. 4: Yes-Setting	23
Hack no. 5: Mirror neurons	26
Hack no. 6: Positive and negative statements	29
Hack no. 7: Presuppositions	32
Hack no. 8: Look into the eyes!	35
Hack no. 9: As-if-frame	38
Hack no. 10: Confirming words	40
Hack no. 11: The echo-technique	42
Hack no. 12: Paraphrasing	45
Hack no. 13: Barnum statements	48
Hack no. 14: Because…	52
Hack no. 15: And then…	56
Hack no. 16: Nationalizations	59

Hack no. 17: Put your preferred option to the end!	62
Hack no. 18: The test drive effect	65
Hack no. 19: Priming	68
Hack no. 20: Pleasure in advance	73
Hack no. 21: Understand their motivation!	75
Hack no. 22: Urgency and shortage	85
Hack no. 23: The lesser of two options	88
Hack no. 24: Constancy	91
Hack no. 25: Just ask, please!	93
Conclusion	95

Hello and welcome to HypnoSale!

This book is about your success in sales by using techniques and strategies from NLP and hypnosis. You will learn basic methods as well as sneaky, nifty tricks for experts. The 25 mental hacks herein will increase your skills and, even more important, your sales. And yes, sometimes the advance you will take from this book may be unfair but I'm pretty sure you deserved it, right?

Anyway, there is no way to make people things they don't want to do generally. So even when equipped with the techniques herein you still need good basic skills and sophisticated, convincing arguments to buy. So bottom line it is still about the quality of your product or service and your knowledge about your offer.

Even if this topic would fill a whole book, we should talk briefly what hypnosis and NLP is and what it's not.

Hypnosis is the art of making the people think whatever you want them to think. But in the end, you can not make them think what they don't want to think at all. So if you are interested in this book because you want to play tricks on others or trick them to buy even if your product is a huge pile of poo, you will be disappointed.

What is NLP? - NLP is for "neurolinguistic programming" which is referring to three things:

"**Neuro**" is for the brain and the psychological and neurological component.

"**Linguistic**" is for the words we use to talk to others and to ourself.

"**Programming**" is the flowchart of our mind and doing.

So NLP is combining psychology, communications, cybernetics and many fields of science more to create a set which can be described best as a " modern psychology".

In this we will combine hypnosis and NLP to give you 25 techniques and strategies to improve your sales skills. That will not make you dispense with the basic skills in sales but giving you additional tools and methods.

If you want to know more about NLP and/or hypnosis, just visit our website **www.nlp-lanka.com** !

Kind regards and best wishes,

Stefan Dittrich

Hack no. 1: Rapport

The first thing we need to talk about is "Rapport".

Maybe you heard about "Rapport" before in a training or in a book, but Rapport is more than just mirroring the gestures.

Rapport means a trustfully, empathic connection between two or more people.

And yes, if you are having good rapport with a person, it's very likely that your mimics and gestures will match, even though it is only a little fragment of rapport.

If there is a positive, strong rapport between two interlocutors, there will be sympathy and an win-win-ambition.

Sure, by learning all the techniques herein, you might be more manipulative. But maybe you gonna use the knowledge to create a win-win-situation with benefits for everyone. Only this way you can ensure a long and prosper customer-relationship.

But let's spend a second more to talk about the seemingly "bad bad manipulation"!

When I have a knife, I can use it to stab someone. But I can use the knife to prepare some food as well. So it's not about the knife.

With fire I can warn a a freezing child. But I also can throw the child into the fire and burn it. So it's not about the fire as well.

I can drink water when I'm thirsty. But if someone made me angry, I can fill up the bathtub and drown him in it. So as you can see it's not about the water, too.

It's only about our intention and the way we use the things and techniques available. it's about how you use the things around you, not about the things itself.

Use the mental hacks herein in this sense! And when creating rapport, you never should try to hard. When you see like someone who desperately tries to mirror the gestures of the interlocutors, people will have a scummy and funky feeling about you. Try to be open, try to feel the others and with creating rapport your intention should be to get an idea about the world what your prospect customer lives in, not about your personal advantage!

3 ways to create rapport:

There are many ways to create good and strong rapport. Increasing the sympathy your interlocutor will feel for you can lead you to a winning situation for both of you.

Here are three of the most common techniques to build rapport:

Physiognomy

To build rapport on a physical base, first of all we use the "Mirroring-Technique" in NLP. That means we are using the same gestures like our partner and we try to reflect the same physiognomy.

Since this can look some kind of weird when the gestures of the interlocutor are to unique, we can use "Cross mirroring". That means we take one specific phenomenon of one channel and reflect it by another one.

By using this cross mirroring we can avoid an uncomfortable feeling caused by a to obvious imitation.

For example we don't want to imitate the nervous clicking with a pen. But we can swing softly with our feet in the same rhythm like our interlocutor is clicking.

Another highly effective way to create rapport on a physical base is the breathing rhythm. When we are breathing in the same depth, rhythm and either in the breast or abdomen, rapport will be created automatically.

Heres another trick: **Drink whenever your interlocutor is raising his or her glass!** This is a very good technique to strengthen the rapport.

VAKOG

Everyone is looking at the world wit different eyes. And one kind of percipience of the world is not the preferred sensual modality of percipience of someone else. That means one person is *seeing* the world while another person is *feeling* what happens. Just because of we can _see_ something clearly doesn't mean somebody else has to _hear_ what you say.

When you hear the words people are saying, you will hear what is their actual preferred channel. They will use different words either they prefer to see what you are talking about, hear what you mean or need to feel that you are right.

These are the different sensual modalities of perception:

- **V**isual ("See", "It looks like", "a clear vision"…)
- **A**uditory ("Listen", "It sounds like", "a strong voice"…)
- **K**inesthetic ("I feel like", "warm person", "deeply touched"…)
- **O**lfactory ("It smells to heaven", "have a good nose"…)
- **G**ustatory ("It's bitter", "You're sweet"…)

Listen to your interlocutors and reflect their sensual modalities! When you hear a prospect customer say: "That **looks** good to me.", you know that it's time to answer: "May I **show you** the **color variations**?". When she says: "I would have a bad **feeling** spending so much money…", you will answer: "You should wear the necklace to **feel how good it feels!**". And "He already **told** me the facts" will automatically provoke a "Well, then **let me say**…".

Meta-Programs

A third way to build strong and stable rapport is by reflecting the "Meta-Programs". This is something you can't learn in many books or courses. This is something from the NLP-Master-Program and maybe unique to this book.

Meta-Programs are special modes we use in thinking, perception and communication. We have different motivations, previous experiences and habits, and so we think and act in different ways. In NLP we use about 30 different Meta-Programs but for this book I took the most important for your use in sales.

Look at your prospect customer and reflect their Meta-Programs to create good rapport!

The most useful Meta-Programs in sales:

- <u>Towards vs. Away</u>
There are people who need to know what they can get out of a business or an investment. They are interested of what is in for them. Others need to know what pain they can avoid by using the product or becoming a costumer. So some people are doing things to become lucky, others are avoiding things to not become unhappy. Both intentions can result to the same outcome.

- <u>Feeling vs. Thinking</u>
Some people need heuristic arguments and rational answers, others need to get a feeling of what you are

talking about and want to actually experience what you have for them.

- Self vs. Others
Some customers are only interested on whats in for them. Others are more empathic in the wealth of everyone and are interested in the benefits for anyone in long term.

- Internal vs. External
Some prospects need to be convinced on their own to be fully committed. Others need an external "go!" (maybe the wife, the boss or someone else).

- Detail vs. Global
Some Interlocutors are interested in details, others want to have a clear picture about the global plan. **Cope their level of interests in details but don't bore them!**

- Sameness vs. Difference
Some people do things because others do. But there are people as well who want to be different in any way. You need to handle if they are interested in important brand ambassadors but you should talk about the unique position if they are more interested in being the only one who knows about this special product.

Practical exercises no. 1

What is your impression of the prospect? Is he or she more about the visual or the auditory information? Maybe kinesthetic, olfactory or gustatory? What are the most relevant modalities to him or her? And why do you think so?

Classify the prospect on this scales!

Visual
Auditory
Kinesthetic
Olfactory
Gustatory

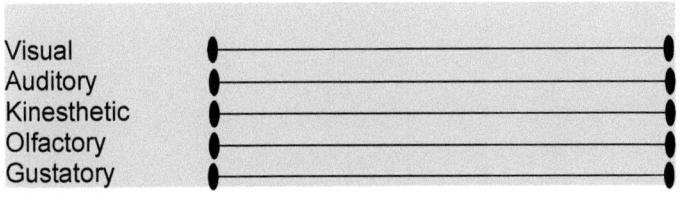

Towards vs. Away
Feeling vs. Thinking
Self vs. Others
Internal vs. External
Detail vs. Global
Sameness vs. Difference

Now that you have got a good feeling for your prospect, give a short teaser about your product or service and why it will meet his or her needs!

Hack no. 2: The "like-me-Drug"

Just imagine, there is a drug, which makes the people liking you!

The good news is: You don't have to imagine. There actually is such a drug.

This is not really a trick from NLP but it is as simple and easy that I just can't keep it for myself! **You'll gonna love this!**

The name of the drug I am talking about is 1,3,7-Trimethylxanthin, it's molecular formula is $C_8H_{10}N_4O_2$ and the structure formula is looking like this:

Perhaps you know it better with its more common name "Caffeine"...

Caffeine is stimulating the brain and this is making to like a person more than without caffeine.

So it's your job to provide enough beverages that contain caffeine!

Sources of caffeine:
- Coffee
- Black tea
- Mate (Paraguay tea)
- Chocolate
- Cocoa
- Guarana
- Energy drinks

Practical exercise no. 2

What source of caffeine do you like most and only if you have an idea: What is the preferred source of caffeine of your prospect (see the list of caffeine-sources above!)?

Hack no. 3: Fake options

When I was working in a mental hospital for ten years, sometimes we had patients, which were not smelling too good. Somehow I had to convince them to take a body wash. But schizophrenic people have very high abilities to blur out things like a bad smell and so they just would say "no" when I would ask them if they would take a shower soon. So I used a nifty trick and asked: "Do you want to take a shower or do you want to use the hot tub?".

As you can see:

Fake options are actual options (!), which all are leading to same intended target.

It is very important to really give them two options! The partner shall actually have two options and be free in his or hers choice! Only the target which both options are leading to is not available as an option.

To me it never made an option weather they took a shower or they did use the hot tub. In the end they would be clean and smelling good...

To use this principle in sales, ask yourself: "What is my intended target?" and find at least two options leading to your goal. Ask your interlocutor which option he or she prefers!

Examples:
- "Do you want to pay cash or with credit card?"
- "Do you know a nice restaurant around here where I can invite you to lunch after we signed the contract?"
- "Do you want to come to my office or shall I come to yours?"
- "Are you available on wednesday in the afternoon or better friday in the morning?"
- "Can I come to your office or do you want me to meet at the fair next week?"

Practical exercise no. 3

What is your intended target?

Find two (or more) options, which are leading to your intended goal! Which are the fake options which all leading to this one intended goal?

Hack no. 4: Yes-Setting

When running for a "Yes", you should make them nod and confirm what you say over and over again before asking the critical question!

As more often your interlocutor will confirm what you say, as less critic he will process the questions. After a few internal or external "yes", it will become a habit to confirm what you are saying.

So before asking the crucial question, **first ask at least three incidental questions which will be confirmed by the prospect customer!**

It's not necessary to do an actual interview. It's also possible to cause internal confirmation and a mental nodding.

Ask the partner things about how he or she came here, about sports, the family or a hobby. Do Small-Talk! You have at least one topic and that is what's making both of you speaking together. So ask him about the sight, the mutual friend, the club, the company or whatever, but **make your prospect customer confirm what you say!**

Examples:

- "Man! That game was awesome!"

- "Isn't he a great piano player?"
- "He is a great person."

- "The sun is no nice today."

- "His PR is great these days."

- "Your family is so nice!"

- "Isn't it sad he passed away last year?"

If something is going wrong and they will not confirm, don't panic! Just start over again!

Practical exercise no. 4

Think about uncritical questions to ask (e.g. "What a great weather, right?") before you will ask the critical question (e.g. "Do you want to see the contract?")! As more as better but you will need at least fife uncritical questions to set up the Yes-Setting.

Hack no. 5: Mirror neurons

Everything started when one scientist stuck out the tongue to a baby chimpanzee. The animal started to stick out his tongue as well and when the scientist made another face, the baby chimpanzee mirrored this again. So neurologists found special brain cells, the "**Mirror neurons**", which are stimulated in our brain when watching somebody else doing something.

Mirror neurons are neurons which create representations of the mental states of others in our brain. When we watch someone doing a thing, we will experience it with a part of our own brain as well.

You know how much it is hurting yourself when watching someone hitting his own thumb with a hammer. Mirror neurons are the suspected reason for why we have to yawn when we see someone else doing it. Or do you know situations when someone else is acting or talking so stupid that you felt embarrassed? And even if this sounds strange but let's face it: Mirror neurons are the reason for porn. There is no other reason why people like watching movies with other people doing it…

Use the principles of the mirror neurons in sales by **subliminal nodding at the question you want to create approval for!**

Be convinced by your product yourself! You only can set people on fire if you are burning first!

Be a kind and open minded person before you want others to be!

Here is a very sneaky trick for sales: **Let him see you signing something!** It doesn't matter what you are signing, just let him or her see! Maybe you sign a credit card slip. Maybe both contracting parties have to sign the contract. It's irrelevant what you are signing but you should do it right in front of the prospects eyes. That will make him feel like signing, too.

Hang up pictures of successful people, happy customers or what ever you want to make them feel. But you also can use this to make them feel insecure when you want to sell injures. In this case you can hang up pictures of burned houses, crashed cars or someone with a plaster cast on this leg...

As a speaker raise your own hand when you want the audience to do so!

And last but not least: **Smile!** That will make them feel happy, too.

Practical exercise no. 5

How can you make your prospects feel in a beneficial way for your intended goal by using the mirror neurons? What can you or others do to make them feel ready to become a customer?

What kind of pictures in your office or in the hallway can be beneficial?

Hack no. 6: Positive and negative statements

There is this myth about us people in NLP that we only want to realize the positive things and blur out the negative. But that's not true. When we're talking about positive and negative statements in NLP, we **don't** talk about **the bottom line of the message.**

A positive statement in the sense of NLP is about **what is** and **what you want**. A negative statement is about what you are **missing** and **what you don't want** to have in your life.

Positive means: "I am...", "I will...", "I wish more ... in my life".

Negative means: "I'm not...", "I won't...", "I wish there is no ... in my life".

So <u>in the sense of NLP (!)</u> the sentence "I'm going to kill myself" is a positive statement while "From tomorrow on there will be no more war in the world" is negative.

Let's do an experiment:

Please think about anything you want. Really anything you want. Nothing is out of limits! But please don't think about a flying elephant.

What did you think about? - Right...

Our mind can not understand if we want something or if we don't want it. The concept of "not" can not be understood by our mind. As long as we are talking about it, it is existing already. At least in our imagination...

In sales you can use this technique in two ways:

1.) Always be aware of negative statements. If there should be positive ask yourself or the interlocutor: "What else **is it**, if it's not...?"!

2.) You also can turn the tide by using tricky negative statements. Don't say: "I'm hoping you will not refuse this offer and ask me to go..."! Better say: "But if you don't want to sign the contract it is o.k. to me as well".

Practical exercise no. 6

What misplaced negative statements do you use? Write those sentences down and find positive statements you can use instead!

Sometimes it can be practical to use negative statements with purpose (e.g. "You don't need to **decide today**" or "It's not necessary to **relax completely**"). What intended use can be beneficial in your business?

Hack no. 7: Presuppositions

Presuppositions are logical units nested inside our statements which are suggesting something while leading the focus of the interlocutor to another logical unit.

Only to think about the sentence means you had to take some nested information as the truth.

Examples:

"Are you interested in our product because of the unique features or because of we have the best support?" → You are interested.

"Do you like the new model because we improved the engine or because of the elegant design?" → You like the new design.

"Is it about the delivery time why you want to change the supplier or is a good bulk discount more relevant to you?" → You want to change the supplier.

When you want to sell more efficiently, use this method in small talk and when presenting the product!

Tell them:

- "When you will enter the red carpet with this dress, there will be a moment of silence for sure..." → *You will wearing this dress.*

- "After using this computer system for half a year, you will have a good idea about how much money it is saving." → *You will use the computer system for half a year.*

- "Do you want to talk about the details of the contract before or after lunch?" → *You want to talk about the details of the contract.*

- "What do you wanna do with all the money you will do with this investment?" → *You will do money with this investment.*

- "See the garden of this real estate! As soon as you are living in here, you can do as much pool parties as you want." → *You will live in here.*

Practical exercise no. 7

What suppositions may be practical in your sales-communication? Ask yourself what facts should be out of question and then nest these facts in another statement (e.g. "Do you think **our product is the best choice** because of the features or the quality?")!

Hack no. 8: Look into the eyes!

People say: "**The eyes are the windows of the soul.**", and it is true.

How much attention do you pay for the eyes of your costumers?

When you will do so from now on, **here is what you can see in the eyes:**

- Emotional level
- Rush vs. constancy
- Affection vs. aversion
- Sensual modality (V, A and K)

Are the pupils **dilated** (mydriasis) or are the pupils **constricted** (miosis) and how do they change as a reaction?

- **Dilated pupils:** sympathy, affection, approval, concentration

- **Constricted pupils:** apathy, aversion, rejection, overload (rapid constriction)

Are the eyes **moving up, down or sidewards**?

- When the pupils are moving **upwards**, your partner is in a visual mode. He is imagine pictures or remembering what he has seen in the past.

- When the pupils move **across to the left or right**, he is focused on the auditory channel. Those people are interested in the informations and want to hear what you have to say.

- When the pupils moving **down**, your interlocutor is perceiving on the kinesthetic channel. Those customers should sit in the car, wear the dress, try the wine...

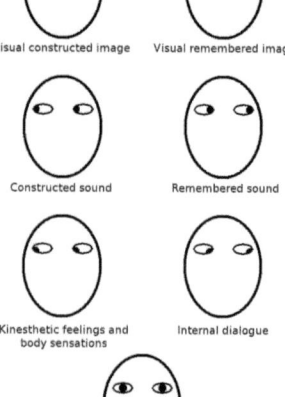

Practical exercise no. 8

Next time you'll going to meet friends, take a few minutes and pay particular attention to their eyes! What do you see? What observations do match the concept? What is different?

Hack no. 9: As-if-frame

In NLP we use the "As-if-frame" which means we pretend for a minute as if our intended goal is reality already.

If you want to unleash the full potential of a person, just treat them now as like you want them to be.

So if you want to make a prospect become a customer, treat him or her like a customer right from the start! Talk to them and act as if they did sign the contract already, as if they bought or as if they will be your partner for years!

You can say:

- "As a member of our club you can use the spa for free."
- "Here is my business card. My customers can call me anytime."
- "Do you have a pen to sign the contract or do you need mine?"
- "I will scan the signed contract and send it via e-mail."

Why you should do like this? Is this some kind of esoteric voodoo? – No, it's not. But it's that simple: When you act by using this "As-if-frame", you are transmitting this concept with all of your communications. Unconsciously your partner will be aware of this confidence and he or she will go with your flow.

Practical exercise no. 9

What is your intended goal in sales (sure, selling. But what else? E.g. happy regular customers, great recommendations, be the best sales person in your company...)? What phrases can you use to work in the sense of the as-if-frame?

How can you behave to work with the as-if-frame nonverbal?

Hack no. 10: Confirming words

Did you ever meet people who are talking like this: "Yes, this is what we have. Good, let's see! Yeah, sure... Well, that looks good!"?

I don't know if those people you've met did know what they are doing or if they had a disorder. But talking like this can be a very nifty trick.

Because hearing someone confirming is enough to be ready to confirm.

Use confirming words or phrases nested in your sentences to provoke confirmation!

When someone is hearing you saying "yes..." or "well..." that will make him confirming more easy as well.

Examples:

- "Yes"
- "You see..."
- "Well"
- "Good"
- "Great"
- "And sure..."
- "As you surely can confirm..."
- "You already said a true thing when ascertained..."
- ...

Practical exercise no. 10

Do you use confirming words like "Well,...", "Good!..." or "Yeah,..."often, sometimes or never? In what situations do you use it?

Try to use these words more often but in a conscious way, not only as expletive words!
What did you find out? What is your résumé?

Hack no. 11: The echo-technique

I'm a member of Toastmasters international since many years and on meetings outside Germany there is this session at the beginning. Everyone has to talk for 30 seconds spontaneously and my first words has to be the last of the person talking before me.

We can use this practice in "HypnoSale" by repeating the last few words of what our partner said. This way you are establishing a bonding with the other person. This technique is especially effective, when this person is running in a auditory mode (VAKOG…).

When using the echo-technique you are repeating keywords used by your interlocutor.

Either you are just repeating slightly while listening with a subliminal nodding or you use the last words of your interlocutor to start your statement.

Example:

A: "What we need is a supplier who can deliver **a huge assortment**."
B: "**A huge assortment** is exactly what you will get with our company."

A: "I don't see **myself in such a car**…"
B: "**You in such a car**? This car seems to be designed to be yours!"

A: "I want to take a look at **the new Prada-Collection**."
B: "**The new Prada-Collection** is right over there..."

A: "I like **the idea**."
B: "**The idea** is is good, right?"

A: "What do you think is **the best option**?"
B: "**The best option** is..."

Practical exercise no. 11

In what typically situations can you use the echo-technique? Make up some examples!

Try this when meeting friends or with your family!

Hack no. 12: Paraphrasing

It's very easy to provoke confirmation when you are listening to people and then just repeat what they have just said. It's really that easy and it is working very well to strengthen the rapport.

Paraphrasing means to **repeat what the interlocutor just said with your own words**.

So in contrast to the echo technique, when using "Paraphrasing" we have to transform the message of our partner to our own language.

For sure that means we have listening very carefully first. Because when you don't get the main message and you are reflecting a wrong statement, you can easily weaken the rapport and loose sympathy.

But here's a trick to prevent messing up by reflecting a wrong message:

Just ask "When I got you right, this is what you think:…" or "Did I get that right?". When asking like this, it will be no problem if you didn't understand the core statement right.

Don't try to overdo when seeking for sophisticated vocabularies. The best paraphrasing is done by your usual words only. As more authentic you are, as better this hack will work.

Examples:

A: "To our company a fast delivery is most important."
B: "So if we will become your supplier, the most important thing to your company will be a fast delivery process. Is that right?"

A: "I have to talk with my wife to make a decision."
B: "So if I understand you correctly, financial decisions is something you and your wife are doing equally, right?"

A: "I'm not sure I have enough information to make a decision right now."
B: "I'm feeling like you need more facts about this offer. Is that correct?"

A: "I know it's awkward but our CEO wants to be involved in all investment decisions. So even if I'm ashamed to admit, but I can't decide on my own."
B: "Now that's a pity! Your CEO really should trust more in your competences. Right?"

The example before is a bit risky indeed, because you are reflecting not the content only but the nested emotions as well. But if you are doing paraphrasing for a while, you will know how to reflect the self-revelation-level correctly.

Practical exercise no. 12

Try to paraphrase the following sentences!

"I'm interested in the data sheet of this car."

"My boss is not happy with our supplier because they don't give quantity discount."

"Those sales representatives are calling every day or coming to my office without an appointment."

"I prefer Linux running on my computer."

"I'm tired of incompetent people on the support-hotline."

Practice paraphrasing with colleagues, family or friends!

Hack no. 13: Barnum statements

There are **statements, which will resonate with most people but still seems very personal**. This way they will fell understood. That is creating a feeling of connection which is generating sympathy and that leads to your sales-success!

> The **Barnum effect**, also called the **Forer effect**, is the observation that individuals will give high accuracy ratings to descriptions of their personality that supposedly are tailored specifically for them but are, in fact, vague and general enough to apply to a wide range of people. This effect can provide a partial explanation for the widespread acceptance of some beliefs and practices, such as astrology, fortune telling, graphology, aura reading and some types of personality tests.
>
> **- Wikipedia -**

Let me tell you about an experiment in 1948. The psychologist Bertram R. Forer gave a sealed envelope to all of his students. He told them, inside is a very scientific analysis of their character and they should read the letter when they got back home and rate it on a scale from 0 to 5.

The next day the students returned and they were exited. Most of them wanted to know how this was possible and how Forer could describe their character that precise. They rated the analysis with 4,26 in average and so they really freaked out when Forer told them, they all had the exact same text.

This is the text they found in the envelope:

> *"You have a great need for other people to like and admire you. You have a tendency to be critical of yourself. You have a great deal of unused capacity which you have not turned to your advantage. While you have some personality weaknesses, you are generally able to compensate for them. Your sexual adjustment has presented problems for you. Disciplined and self-controlled outside, you tend to be worrisome and insecure inside. At times you have serious doubts as to whether you have made the right decision or done the right thing. You prefer a certain amount of change and variety and become dissatisfied when hemmed in by restrictions and limitations. You pride yourself as an independent thinker and do not accept others' statements without satisfactory proof. You have found it unwise to be too frank in revealing yourself to others. At times you are extroverted, affable, sociable, while at other times you are introverted, wary, reserved. Some of your aspirations tend to be pretty unrealistic."*

Forer explained he just took some phrases from some horoscopes he bought at a bookstore in front of his house.

What is there to learn from this?

There are statements, which will resonate with most people but still seems to be very personal. This way they will feel understood which will create a feeling of connection. So Barnum statements will generate sympathy and that is leading to your sales-success!

Examples:

"You are an independent thinker and you will not accept others' statements without satisfactory proof. So I will give you the information you'll need and then you will decide on your own..."

"I'm sure security is one of your major goals in life and this product is the ultimate solution to achieve this goal."

"I think you have a good feeling for people who just want to take benefits and the others who are interested in a win-win-situation."

"Sometimes it's hard to make the right decision and often the even bigger dilemma is that there are pro and cons for all of the options. Right?"

Tip: Read horoscopes and analyze the statements for useful phrases!

Practical exercise no. 13

Please go to the shop and get a newspaper or a book with horoscopes. Read it and try to adept the statements to use it in your meetings!

Hack no. 14: Because…

Do you know the favorite word of little children? It's a word, that almost all parents hate like death until their kid is fife years old. The word I'm writing about is "Why?".

There's a time in any toddler's life, when they just can't stop asking "Why…? Why…? Why…?". Even if this is funny in the beginning, it will make you go crazy after a few minutes.

Anyway this phase in growing up is a perfect demonstration of the humans urge to have explanations. We want to know the causal relationships in this world and, believe it or not, these causes don't need to be logical all the time.

Humans feel an urge for reasons and explanations. No one wants to be irrational.

If there is no obvious reason people will search for ANY reasons or make explanations up.

So in order to prevent adverse explanations, you better give reasons to your interlocutors.

You can't believe there is no need for logical explanations? – Sure, it is even better if you can give rational causes, but in the end it doesn't matter how good or weak it is.

Scientists did an experiment and asked people waiting in the line of a Xerox machine if they may jump the queue.

First they tried by asking: "Excuse me, I have five pages. May I use the Xerox machine?".

Faced with this direct request and no given explanation to cut ahead in the line, exactly 60% of the people agreed.

Than they retried the experiment by asking: "May I use the Xerox machine, because I'm in a rush?".

So this time they gave the people a reason, "…because I'm in a rush…". Even if they didn't change anything but the phrase, this time almost everyone complied. To be more exact: 94% of the people in the line accepted.

You see what happened? Only by using the word "because", only by giving an explanation, a third more of the people gave the permission to jump the queue.

You doubt that it is because of the cause? You think it's more relevant that the reason was plausible? The people in the line just respected the leakage of time to wait…? - No. The scientists did a third run.

This time they asked: "May I use the Xerox machine, because I have to make copies?"

Really?! You really need to use the Xerox machine because you have to make copies? Now who would guess that?...

As you can see, this is maybe the most stupid explanation to jump the queue when waiting to use a Xerox machine.

This time, with the most senseless explanation, still almost everyone accepted. Only one per cent less let the experimenter pass (93% in total), even with this nonsense explanation.

So no matter how good or bad your reasons are, always give an cause to your interlocutors!

Examples:

"And because you understand the future markets, you will be very happy with buying thin product."

"I'm sure you're already aware about the high quality of our products because Mr. Smith recommended our company."

"Your wife will be proud of you, because this is the best choice."

Practical exercise no. 14

Think about what you want the other person to do, think or say! And now make up reasons why they should act or this way (remember: this reasons don't need to be logical…)!

Hack no. 15: And then…

We are living in a world of options and my personal mind is that this is good. But since it became too many options in our modern western society, people tend to accept when we are giving them structure and procedural processes.

I think most people will disagree to seeking for procedures but options, because they like the idea of being free of will. But there is so much option in life, sometimes we like to give the control to someone else.

Chain one command to another to establish a procedure!

There is no guarantee that they will take your order without putting up resistance. Sometimes they will disagree and resist, but just as well there's a good chance they will appreciate your offer and accept what you are saying.

Examples:

"First we should do the paperwork and then I will introduce you to John."

"Let me show you the technical specifications and then you should do a test drive."

"Here's my plan for today: First I will show you our product, then I will do you the numbers on what you will save. Then we can talk about the contract and then I have a little surprise for you..."

"Welcome! Be my guest and have some refreshments at the bar! First we will have a little come-together and then we will start the meeting fully motivated."

"Try it by yourself and then you will find out how easy it is to use."

Practical exercise no. 15

Think about what you want the other person to do, think or say! And now make up a procedural pattern to get him or her out of to many options!

Hack no. 16: Nationalizations

Now I want to show you a special an important kind of words.

These words are declared do be nouns but they are not. In school we learned, substantives are words about things you can touch or at least see. Nouns are material things but the words I'm writing about here are not. It's about "NOMINALIZATIONS".

> *In linguistics, [...] nominalization is the use of a word which is not a noun [...] as a noun.*
> ### - Wikipedia -

When we use nominalizations, we **transform individual processes and experiences into a word**. This way we don't have to specify what our interlocutor will feel or think about what we are talking about.

There is no love or did you ever see or touch some material object called "love"? There is no freedom or can you show this thing to me? We simplified a set of circumstances or an individual process that we could think it is a substantive. But it is not!

"Love", "freedom" or "bliss" are stopgap solutions to have a certain word for complex and abstract processes and circumstances. It doesn't matter what "love" is to someone, what feelings he will feel when he is in love and if he is making associations with "romance" or rather with "sex".

You don't know exactly what your partner is thinking of when you talk about "love". But the good news is: You don't need to know when using nominalizations.

We can't say anything wrong with nominalizations because anyone can have his or hers own ideas when listening to you.

But there's even more about nominalizations:

To examine the accuracy of your statement, the interlocutor has to activate his personal process behind the nominalization and compare it with the actual situation. But since they pushed the specific button in their brain just a second before, they will find out that this feeling is real, just like magic. That means: Only talking about happiness will make the people happier.

And just to mention: As better you make a person feel, as bigger is the sympathy, as better is your chance that he or she will become your customer.

Examples for nominalizations:
- Success
- Joy
- Happiness
- Love
- Luck
- ...

Practical exercise no. 16

What nominational words can make your interlocutors more open to your arguments?

Hack no. 17: Put your preferred option to the end!

It might sound pessimistic but this is only realistic. Here is a very important principle for your success in sales with hypnosis:

People are lazy and people don't listen.

If there's not a very important reason, people will take the easiest way and the line of the least resistance.

Read carefully: "If there's not a very important reason…"! When your options seem to have the same amount of pros and cons or possibilities vs. risks, your interlocutor really has no idea which option to pick and so he is (unconsciously) looking for an easy way to get out of this dilemma.

This is why this hack is working: **Repeating your last words is the most easy and efficient way to pick an option.**

When you prefer to meet a person on Friday in the morning, you should ask: "Do you want to meet on Wednesday in the afternoon or do prefer Friday at 11 a.m.?"!

Or you can say: "Do you want us to deliver the car to your home or do you want to come here to drive home with your new car?"

Again: If there is a good reason for your customer to choose option no. 1, this hack may possibly not work. But the proof of the pudding is in the eating, so just try it!

Putting your preferred option to the end will increase the chance your interlocutor will chose this.

Practical exercise no. 17

What options are you giving to your interlocutors? And how can you give them the choice within putting your preferred option to the end? Write down some example phrases!

Hack no. 18: The test drive effect

Do you know the cliché of the pusher who will give you the first shoot for free?

Someone who doesn't know your product simply can't know what a good feeling it is to use it, how good it suits him or her and how jealous the neighbors will become. They just don't know the good feeling and how much benefits will come with being your customer.

But there's a very simple solution to this problem:

Let them drive the car!
Let them sit in the massage chair!
Let them wear the jewelry!
Let them use the system in their company!
Just LET THEM DO IT!

They will remember what good feeling it had been to wear the dress, the jewelry, drive the car, use the system... and they will wish to have this in their life constantly.

No matter what your service or product is, there should always be a way to test whatever you want to sell.

If you've just opened a restaurant, let the people try your food! Maybe you prepare some special finger-food and give it to the people who are passing by your restaurant.

Just the other week I received a box of 12 sachets with a nutritional supplement for recreation when you have a hangover. I met the guys with **"one:47"** last year at a fair and we wanted to try their anti-hangover-drink but that time they just had prototypes of the bottles. Now that they released their product they mailed a free box. I tried it and I really like that stuff, even without having a hangover.

So no matter what you're offering: **Always make sure there is a free trial-version or the chance to try it one time.** The chance that people will buy after a test-drive is much better than without any test.

Practical exercise no. 18

What are you offering? What is your main-product and what are the up-sell-products? How and in what way can you offer the prospect customers a free trial or sample of what you got for them?

Hack no. 19: Priming

To understand the next hack, I have to reveal one of the biggest secrets in mind-reading:

The most difficult but also most important thing in mind-reading is not the reading part. It's the part when we put the thought to their mind first we want to read. Because a lot of the tricks are based on this concept:

First we make them thinking about the things we want, and then "read" their mind.

Most people will not be aware the way we put our ideas to their mind. They will be astonished how precise you could tell what they were thinking about, but they don't realize that you putted this thought there just a few seconds before.

The technique we are using to put an idea to someone's mind is called "Priming".

> *"Priming is an implicit memory effect in which exposure to one stimulus [...] influences the response to another stimulus."*
> *- Wikipedia -*

Let's do a very simple Priming-Example:

Think about a lucky dwarf!

And now think about any one-digit number that comes spontaneously to your mind!

Is it seven? - How comes?

To eliminate the possibility you just said seven because you saw it on the page, I will explain the trick on the next page…

Solution to the "luck-dwarf-routine":

It's very easy because I pushed the seven to your mind. I told you to think about a lucky dwarf.

Maybe it's depending on the environment you grow up in, but most societies think about the 7 as a **lucky number**. And I also don't know if you grow up with the ferrytales of the Grimm-brothers but there is a very famous story about "**Snow White and the seven dwarfs**". So if you know about both of this associations I'm pretty optimistic you had "7" on your mind when I made you thinking about a **lucky dwarf** first.

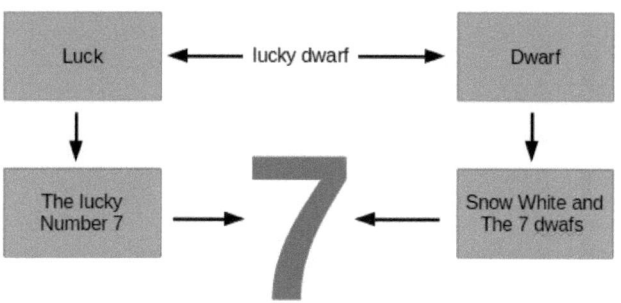

You could be even more sure it will be the seven if you make them think about a lucky dwarf who is drinking a lemon soda (7up), a lucky dwarf who is a sailor (the seven seas) or anything else that is associated with the number seven.

Examples for priming in sales:

- Hot beverages
This is warming peoples heart / stomach and making them more kind.

- Comfortable seats
This will relax their body and soul.

- Luxury environment
They will feel more successful.

- Status symbols
They will be more focused on wealth.

- Happy and successful customers
The customers seems happy and so I will be...

- Cash
Researches did recover, people will be more generous and less stingy.

- Signatures
When people will be exposed to signatures, they will be more motivated to give your own signature.

- ...

Practical exercise no. 19

Think about what you want to make your interlocutors to do or think! Write it down!

You can do some research on Google or YouTube by searching for "Priming".
And now write down some ideas about how to use this technique in sales! Don't censor your ideas! Write down everything coming to your mind!

Hack no. 20: Pleasure in advance

Do a <u>REAL</u> favor for your prospect customer and let him or her be in-debt to you!

People don't want to owe a favor to others and so if you will do a pleasure to your prospect in advance, that will make them more open to your arguments and lead the path to make them a customer because they want to balance the debt.

But as you can see by my underlining above it should be a **real** favor! That's very important, because if you give them just a promotional pen or something like that, it is nothing they really appreciate. So when I'm writing about a favor, I mean something that really shows you know what is important to this specific person.

Sometimes it is just about a useful item for their hobby. Sometimes it is about a very useful contact you gave them. It just should not be any random gift. Always take care it's something individual and something your prospect really needs and appreciates.

Do research about what they like. Use the internet! Use the company's website, social medias, ask friends and business partners or the assistant! Ask those people: "I want to make a gift to… Do you have any idea what he is into?"

Practical exercise no. 20

Now actually do research about your key-partners or a proposal customer and find out what they are into! How can you use this information to do a real pleasure or a useful gift to them! Write it down!

Hack no. 21: Understand their motivation!

People are individuals. And since they are so, there are many different motivators. A motivator that will make one person work like a maniac doesn't mean anything to others.

Psychology claimed to found out there are 14 different motivators. All of them are different and all of them have different meaning to the individual. So if you're looking for ways to sell more efficiently, you should know about the following motivators.

The possible main motivators of people are:

1. Being active and engaged
People who are responding to this motivator, appreciate the feeling of being engaged. they hate to have free time and you will make them the most happy people when you can provide them appointments or heavy workload.

2. Responsibility
Those people are liking the feeling to being needed and responsible.

3. Past achievements
People with this motivator want to look back in time and see what he or she accomplished in the past.

4. Attractive environment
Who is responding to this motivator is very much into a beautiful surrounding. This people need to be in an attractive environment to know they did well.

5. Perceptible progress / results
With this motivator I can remember a friend of my trainer. He had been an academic philosopher before becoming a wall-painter. Nobody could understand why he gave up an academic career to paint walls. When people asked him why he did so he answered: "When I go home in the evening I can turn around and watch the walls. In the morning they had been white, now they are red. So I know my life matters.". - And this is exactly what motivates a person with this motivator... more then status or the reputation.

6. Companionship
There are people who will get motivated by the common feeling with others. Those people like to be a part of a group and they want to feel connected.

7. Challenge
Other people want to push themselves to the limit over and over again. Only when they are breaking their own limitations, they will be happy.

8. Competition
There are people who get motivated the most when they know they are in a competition with others. "Who is the most...?", "Who is the most successful...?" or "Who has the biggest...?" - That is what makes this people tick.

9. Recognition
People who are running with this motivator like to be seen as "the most important person of ..." or "the true expert on ...". Those people appreciate to have fans and to be seen as an expert on their field.

10. Preparation
This kind of person wants to have the idea to be prepared well. It doesn't matter if the case of emergency will ever come. But such people need the idea to be prepared for whatever there will come. Some kind it's a sort of security but even if they will never need their knowledge, they will be happy by the thought to be prepared only.

11. Living your beliefs
There are people who are ready to die for their convictions. If they are convinced that something is not right, they rather will die instead of betraying their ideals. Those people will be motivated when you will give them a chance to live their believes.

12. Having visions and dreams
Those peoples are burning for their visions. They will give anything to see their dreams come true. It's important to give them a vision and as soon this vision became reality you should hold another for them.

13. Role models
Those people care about what their idols do. There really has to be no other reason, but since their role models did like that, they will be open to do as well.

14. Audience
And last but not least there are people who do things because others are watching. Those people really appreciate the audience. As more, as better.

3 to 5 of those motivators are dominant to any person. Those we call the "**Main motivators**". If you want to make people tick, you should find out what their personal main motivators are and **tell them how your offer will help to satisfy these needs**.

How can you know what are the relevant motivators to a person?

- Listen to them!
They will tell you about the exiting things in their life. No matter what they will tell you, always think about what motivator this is pointing to!

- Take a close look!
People have stuff in their office. Look at the pictures in their office or at the pictures they are putting on their desk. No matter if it is a picture of their dog or a trophy they won with their soccer-team, those things do mean a lot to them, otherwise it wouldn't be there. These indications can give you a good idea about their motivators.

- Do research!
We are living in modern times. You can find almost any information on the internet. And even if there are many

people who think this is bad at all, I think there are some benefits as well. You can do research on the internet, by using social medias, call and ask friends or the assistant of your interlocutor. Try to reveal what is important to a prospect customer and always try to find out what motivator can be important for him or her!

So when you want to use this model of motivators to increase your sales, you should do this three-steps-program:

1. Do your homework (→ Research)!

2. Define the main motivators!

3. Tell them how your product or service will help them to achieve at least one of those motivators (better all of them...)!

Practical exercise no. 21

Find reasons to become your customer for any motivators!

1. Being active and engaged

2. Responsibility

3. Past achievements

4. Attractive environment

5. Perceptible progress / results

6. Companionship

7. Challenge

8. Competition

9. Recognition

10. Preparation

11. Living your beliefs

12. Having visions and dreams

13. Role models

14. Audience

Hack no. 22: Urgency and shortage

When your prospect is convinced in general but a "last push" is needed to make him / her a customer, it's a good idea to create a limitation to your product or service.

Again this is a technique which is working best, when your prospect is convinced already. Otherwise you might seen scummy! So wait to use this hack until you're thinking there is just one last reason needed!

You can limit your offer…

- by time.
- by available amount.
- by extras included.
- to this particular person.
- …

This will cause a certain feeling of urgency and as soon they are convinced they will know there is no time to waste, otherwise this extra-surperb offer will be gone.

Examples:

"When you decide until the end of the month, I can get you the extended warranty for free."

"I can reserve three of this for two weeks. But since this is a hot product, I can't book more or longer for you."

"Please note that this offer is restricted to you exclusively! I can give this offer to you and maybe to your partners, but it is strictly restricted."

"Decide today and I will give you 25% as a discount."

Practical exercise no. 22

How can you put limitation to your product? Think about the different possibilities of limitation!

Hack no. 23: The lesser of two options

Did some of your friends asked you to help moving ever? If so, what did you reply? Did you carry the heavy boxes and furniture or did you have an excuse?

If this friends would really care about your feelings they would take care for you are helping AND feeling good with it. But there is more: If they would know this book, they would be able to make even more people helping them. How? - It's very easy...

How to make people help you moving...

1. Ask people to lend you the money for the security deposit.

2. They will refuse it with many excuses.

3. Say: "OK, I can understand. But can you help me moving?"

4. They will help because they are happy to help with such a small effort (compared to the lending of money) and they feel guilty already. So they want to balance the refuse before.

Maybe this seems to be emotional blackmail to you but this technique is very efficient. Once they refused something you had been asking for, they will feel the urge to balance this. So the possibility to say "yes" the next time is more likely.

If you want to make people saying "yes", you should make sure they said "no" the first time!
Examples:

A: "Can you give me the number of your boss? So I can tell him."
B: "No, I'm sorry but that's not possible."
A: "O.k., I can understand. But perhaps I can show it to you…?"
B: "Hmm, all right."

A: "This car with all the extras will cost 125.000$."
B: "Uhh, that's much!"
A: "The basic-version is available for only 55.000$."
B: "That's what I'm looking for."

Practical exercise no. 23

What requests can you make before asking them the critical question to use this technique?

Hack no. 24: Constancy

But there is even more! **Once you've made a person say "yes" to your offer, it is very likely they will say "yes" the next time again.**

Why is that?

It is because people want to look constant. No one wants to seem irrational and so they will made up any explanations for their first "yes", so now they will have a cause to say "yes" again. Otherwise they will need very good explanations why they accepted the last time but refuse now. And because this explanation will be hard to find it is more easy to say "yes" the next time as well.

People have the tendency to redo things for you, once they did the first time.

You can use this concept when approaching a regular costumer. Just ask him for **another** meeting or to trust in you **again**! Let them remember that they met you before or that they bought your product before. So they will know it would be irrational to trust you once but not this time.

Ask people to do things "… again"!

Practical exercise no. 24

Write down your most potential customers from the past!

And now think about what you can ask them to do **again** or if there is **another** good deal for them!

Hack no. 25: Just ask, please!

The last hack on this program is just as easy as it is hard.

People today don't learn to ask for something and they feel weak when saying "please". But what those people miss is the might of a friendly request.

Our upbringing and education taught us to be friendly and helpful. So that way we are trained to help if somebody is asking for.

When other people will hear "Please!" or "Can you help me please? …!", they will try their best to be helpful.

No matter how sure a shot seems to you, **kindly ask your prospect to do whatever you want them to do!**

Examples:

"Would you please sign here!"

"Could you give me his telephone number, please!"

"Please give me the chance to show you our product!"

"Excuse me please!..."

"Can you help me please?..."

Practical exercise no. 25:

Think about what you really want your interlocutor to do! Write down how you can ask them to do this favor to you!

Now do training and ask people for favors! Say "Please" and "Can you help me?" as much as possible! As more practice you will have as better you will do when it is a *real Situation*.

Conclusion

Now you are ready to go. You learned the theoretical part of **HypnoSale** and you did some practical exercises. But sales is about doing it. As more appointments you had and as more practical experience you made, as more effective you will sell.

Take the hacks out of this book and try to realize one by one, meeting by meeting and I'm more than optimistic that you will sell more efficiently.

If you want to learn more about NLP in business or personal context or you want to learn about the core-techniques on hypnosis, just visit our website:

www.nlp-lanka.com

Please give me feedback and maybe some good recommendations If you are satisfied!

I'm wishing you the best from my heart and I hope to have the chance to meet you in person some day.

Kind regards, best wishes. Love and Peace,

Stefan Dittrich

P.S.: If you want to learn more about HypnoSale, just tun over to the next page...

This program is also available as a video-course at

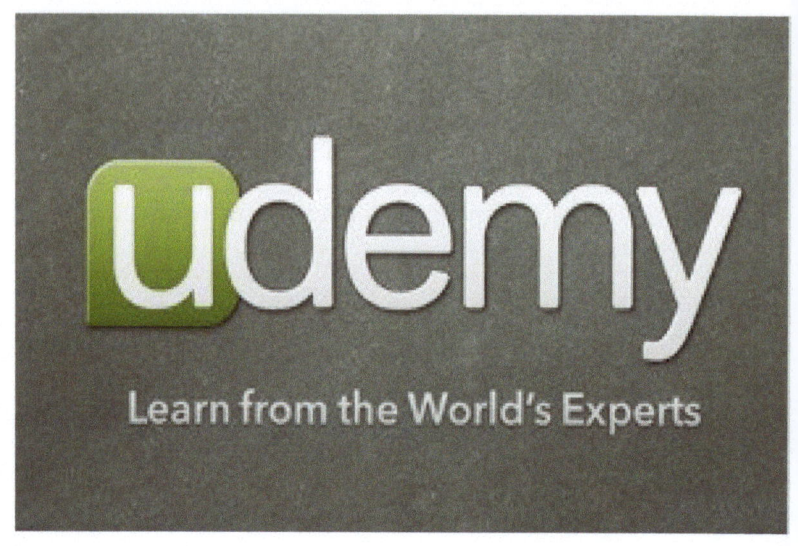

To learn more just visit
www.udemy.com
and search for:

HypnoSale
NLP and HYPNOSIS in SALES

25 mental HACKS for your
SUCCESS in SALES

See you there... ;)